Stupid Poems 11

Stupid Poems 11

Ian Vannoey

Matador
9 Priory Business Park,
Wistow Road, Kibworth Beauchamp,
Leicestershire. LE8 0RX
Tel: (+44) 116 279 2299
Fax: (+44) 116 279 2277
Email: books@troubador.co.uk
Web: www.troubador.co.uk/matador

ISBN 978 1784621 940

British Library Cataloguing in Publication Data.
A catalogue record for this book is available from the British Library.

Typeset by Troubador Publishing Ltd, Leicester, UK

Matador is an imprint of Troubador Publishing Ltd

Contents

Smelly Europeans

(when Europeans first landed in Japan in the sixteenth
century, the Japanese found them rather smelly).

If you ask me what I think
Of Europeans – well, they stink.
You can tell them in a jiffy,
As you'll find they're rather whiffy.
I've begun to give up hope
That they would start using soap.
I really don't think very much
Of the hygiene of the Dutch.
As regards the Portuguese;
I cannot sit with them with ease.
When a Spaniard comes along,
I always think: 'What a pong!'
I'm afraid your average Brit
Smells just like a pile of shit.
You can always tell the French,
As they make such a stench.
It seems that each Italian
Is really, really, really smelly and
It also seems that every Hung-
-Arian smells like dung.
Why is every Latvian
Always rather flatulen-
T? The Poles, the Danes, the Swiss, the Greeks,
And everyone in Europe reeks.

Why is a living room called a living room?

If a living room is for living,
Other rooms are for being dead in.

Ode to titanium

Titanium's light, titanium's strong.
With titanium you can't go wrong.
It's not reactive and it doesn't rust.
Using titanium is a must.
Seventeen hundred degrees – it's melting point.
It makes a great artificial joint.
Titanium is really great.
Forty-eight is its atomic weight.
'Titanium' sounds good, which is why they make
'Titanium' golf clubs which are quite fake.
It's used in jets and it's used in rockets.
To buy titanium you need deep pockets.
To seek cheap titanium is quite futile.
It's found in a mineral that's called rutile.
Let's raise our voices; let's all sing.
Of all metals titanium's king.

Is the Pope a foot fetishist?

(the Pope caused surprise recently when, in a ceremony in which he washed people's feet, women were included for the first time)

Our spirituality makes us whole.
I'm concerned about your sole.
For this gift the Lord we thank – all
Women have a shapely ankle.
There are millions in my flock.
I can get inside their sock.
Why is it that, do you suppose,
Almighty God created toes,
And also insteps, and the heel,
And made the foot have such appeal?
A woman's beauty's not complete
Unless she has lovely feet.

The well-endowed whale

The right whale has an amazing feature:
The biggest penis of any creature.
This was said by a right whale lady:
"Is that a tree-trunk or are you pleased to see me?"

La Vida Breve

A notable opera that was written in Spain.
There really aren't so many (you can say that again!)
If you do not like this opera by Manuel de Falla,
You must admit that it is a powerful piece of drama.
Poor gypsy girl Salud is madly in love
With Paco, who's in a social class above.
She suffers so much when he's a little late.
Granny and Uncle Salvador both lament her fate.
The vicissitudes of fate have conspired to damn 'er.
'Cursèd are they born anvil and not hammer'.
From his own social class, Paco's found a bride.
Salud has just been a plaything on the side.
Uncle Salvador wants to kill Paco on the spot.
He's restrained by Granny, who laments Salud's lot.
Salud's completely shattered, and she is aghast,
That Paco's found a wife from a higher social class.
Desperate, she and Salvador decide to gatecrash
The singing, dancing people at Paco's wedding bash.
They confront Paco, who's cheated and he's lied.
Salud takes a knife, and commits suicide.

A typical phone call

'The first thing we must say is:
This call is recorded for training purposes.
Press one to save the nation.
Press two if you're dying from frustration.
Press three if visions you are seeing.
Press four to talk to a human being.
All our advisers are occupied.
We hope you're not committing suicide.
Your call is important to us so
It has been placed in a queue.
We're so sorry to keep you waiting.
Here's some music that's irritating.'
Half an hour passes by.
You've better ways to spend the day.
But then, the greatest of all joys.
You get to hear a human voice.
Your heart leaps in exultation.
At last an end to your frustration.
'How is it I can help today?'
'I've forgotten what I was going to say'.

La Traviata

It may be that opera is really not your thing.
But in Verdi's popular work you'll know some tunes they sing.
Violetta is a courtesan (a sort of high-class whore),
But then she meets Alfredo, and couldn't love him more.
They live together in the country, and they're very happy.
But then she gets a visit from Alfredo's pappy,
Who tells her that, sadly, she will have to break
The relationship, for Alfredo's family's sake.
She can't tell him face-to-face, so she writes a letter.
Alfredo is incensed to get this from Violetta.
He insults her publicly, when they're at a function.
Little does he know that she's dying from consumption.
They're finally reconciled, in the end when she's dying,
But being on her death-bed doesn't stop her singing.

There aren't many people called Arthur around these days

Something that is really hard: yer
Look for someone who's called Arthur.
Of all the people you have met,
There is no Arthur I would bet.
Your mates are Kevin, Dave and Chris.
There is no Arthur on the list.
In the time of my father,
Lot's of people were called Arthur.
Now it is a rarity
To find an Arthur under ninety.
Other names for which the same is
True are Reg, Stan and Mavis.
The following names are still more rare:
Lancelot and Guinevere.

IAN VANNOEY

My best friend is a lamp post

My best mate is really tall.
Beside him, everyone is small.
He's also very, very slim.
He's very bright; he is not dim.
His conversation is not great,
But he does illuminate.
He likes to hang out in the street.
A quieter chap you just can't meet.
He's always at his best at night.
Whenever we are in a fight
He's very, very, very tough.
I lean on him when I feel rough.
He isn't very good at fishing,
But as a friend he is quite spiffing.

The Rite of Spring

In Paris, back in 1913,
A strange new ballet was, for the first time, seen.
It was not watched in peace and quiet.
It very nearly sparked a riot.
The Ballets Russes performed in France.
They'd flocked to see Nijinsky dance.
But it was different, this new thing.
There was nothing like The Rite of Spring.
Scenes of Pagan Russia was the theme.
So strange and savage it would seem.
With strange new music by Stravinsky,
And weird choreography by Nijinsky.
The rhythm changes in every bar.
Count the time – you won't get far.
Some thought it an abomination.
Some thought 'a great creation'.
They screamed and shouted at each other.
And music would be changed for ever.

Dinner with the England cricket team

If you have no Prior engagement, when the Bell rings for dinner, Trott along to the dining room where the Cook (And 'er son) have prepared roast Swann with Onions, Root vegetables and Broad beans.

The Islets of Langerhans

(if you studied Biology at school, you might know that the
Islets of Langerhans are in the pancreas)

I love to lay upon the sands
Of the Islets of Langerhans.
This is the place to take your ease.
The palm trees sway in the breeze.
The sun shines from a clear blue sky.
Friendly natives all say 'Hi!'.
On the shore the waves lap gently,
And after dark the nights are balmy.
So hurry then, do not delay.
To travel agent, make your way.
The best vacation destination
Is part of your digestive system.

The panda's recipe book

Table of contents
The end

Disorganised Crime

This bank raid was a total cock-up.
We'll all end up in the lock-up.
If you want to commit crime,
It helps if you turn up on time.
To patiently join the queue
Was a silly thing to do.
Sawn-off shotguns serve their end
If you saw off the right end.
My balaclava hid me well;
I'd left my name on my lapel.
Our organization was not great:
The getaway car turned up late.
We were really out of luck:
In heavy traffic it got stuck.
Next time that a bank we'll rob,
We'll try to do a proper job.

IAN VANNOEY

Homosexual Composers

Pyotr Tchaikovsky had to conceal
That women, for him, had no appeal.
(From what I hear, for those who are gay,
It's much the same in Russia today).
Britten lived with Peter Pears.
In their time they were thought 'queers'.
Tippett wrote The Midsummer Marriage.
But then there was no gay marriage.
Poulenc combined spirituality
With homosexuality.
Camille Saint-Saëns was also French.
He had no interest in any wench.
We'll cross the Atlantic, for the next is
Bernstein, who liked both sexes.
From great cowboy music you'd never say
Aaron Copland was Jewish and gay.
Another American who used to harbour
Gay inclinations was Samuel Barber.
While on Americans I s'pose we oughtta
Make a mention of Cole Porter.
It's sad to think that in their time
The way they lived was then thought crime.

16

Why is your bottom called your bottom?

The bottom of most things to be found
Somewhere that's close to the ground.
If your bottom were in you feet,
That would be a name that's neat,
But your bottom is not found
Anywhere that's near the ground.
Your bottom is almost three feet up.
Why's it called this? I give up.
A better term would be 'behind',
For round the back your bottom you'll find.
If you're standing on your head,
Your head is at the bottom instead.
This is a name that's really rotten.
Why is your bottom called your bottom?

Comparison Sites

If of car insurance you're a buyer,
Hotels or energy supplier,
The thing to do that's just right
Is go to a comparison site.
A few minutes at your computer
Will quickly find the deal to suit yer.
But how do you find the comparison site,
That, for you, is just right?
There are many comparison sites.
There should be comparison sites
Which compare comparison sites.
But if there are comparison sites
Which compare comparison sites,
There could be comparison sites
Which compare comparison sites
Which compare comparison sites.
This poem now must reach its end,
As I'm going round the bend.

Thoughts in the dentist's waiting room

(inspired by the 'Nightmare song' from Gilbert and Sullivan's 'Iolanthe')

Though it's just a check-up, I do get so het up; I do hope I
    won't have a filling.
It seems quite pathetic for he'll use anaesthetic but I hate it
    whenever he's drilling.
To say I'm not taxed, that I am quite relaxed, whenever I come
    to the surgery,
That it's all in my stride, then I would have lied; I would be
    committing perjury.
It would be more fun to be out in the sun for it's springtime
    with flowers and buds.
For it does seem at last that the winter has passed with its
    winds and its storms and its floods.
My appointment's at ten, but I don't know when I'll be asked
    to go in by the nurse.
I really am hating this very long waiting and each time it
    seems to get worse.
Those two little boys are making such noise, each rushing
    around like a hooligan.
They really must learn, their mum should be stern, and tell
    them to sit on their stool again.
There's mags in a pile so patients can while away the time
    and read while they wait.

But they are so boring, they're well worth worth ignoring, on
   reading I can't concentrate.
That nurse is attractive, my mind's overactive, I do hope I
   wasn't caught staring.
I'm a dirty old sod, I must seem quite odd, but right now I'm
   really past caring.
I surely am next, I'm getting quite vexed, I'm the last person
   left in the room.
My turn's come at last, the waiting is past, I'll go in to meet
   my doom.

Poem about satellite dishes in the style of Wordsworth's 'Daffodils'

I wandered lonely on my bike
And there beheld a wonder, which is,
Standing clearly as you like,
A host of greyish satellite dishes.

Pointing upwards to the sky,
It really was a sight to see,
They pointed upwards, that is why
The folks inside get Sky TV.

Upon each house, high on a wall,
Their angle had to be just right,
They were directed so they all
Pointed to the satellite.

You'll watch your favourite programmes when
They have installed it with no fuss.
You can watch them there and then
Or record them with Sky Plus.

And when your dish is in position,
So on the satellite it locks,
You'll watch in high definition,
If you have an HD box.

Each one's a nice parabola.
If you've not got one you must wish
That very soon you will be having a
Really lovely satellite dish.

Faust

Many writers and composers have felt that they would fail
If they did not write their own special version of this tale.
Here are some names that are on quite a long list:
Marlowe and Goethe, Gounod, Berlioz and Liszt.
Dr. Faust is a scholar, he's alone in his room.
He's bored and depressed, and all is doom and gloom.
Along comes Mephistopheles, who is, of course, Satan.
And he says to Faust: 'You're not feeling great and
I'll give you all you want; you'll be young again.
I'll just want your soul, so sign with this pen'.
So Faust says 'okay'; they go off to a hostelry,
Where they join in the fun, the singing and the revelry.
Mephistopheles feels that this is not enough,
So he fixes Faust up with a lovely piece of stuff.
In some versions she's called Gretchen, in others Marguerite.
No matter what she's called, she's virtuous and sweet.
Mephistopheles conjures up a fiendish piece of devilry.
He puts in Gretchen's room a lovely box of jewellery.
Gretchen falls for Faust, hook, line, and sinker.
To keep her mum quiet, she gives her to drink a
Dose of sleeping draught, but rather overdoes it.
Her mother drinks too much, whereupon she snuffs it.
Gretchen gets pregnant, which precipitates her fall.
This pleases Mephistopheles (he's the Devil after all).
She disposes of her baby, so to hide her shame.

23

(Back in the nineteenth century, she'd get all the blame).
So she goes to prison, awaiting execution.
But she still goes to Heaven, and achieves salvation.
Does Faust go to Hell? Where does he go to?
This depends on the version, so I'll leave that to you.

If you only have one chopstick you can't eat Chinese food but there are other things you can do with it

Chinese food is not much fun
If of chopsticks you've just one.
You can only sit and glower
At your plate of sweet and sour.
Just one chopstick isn't nice
If you're faced with egg fried rice.
A single chopstick all forlorn
Cannot cope with a king prawn.
What can you do with just one chopstick?
Conduct the London Philharmonic.
Another thing to do, I think,
Is use it to unblock a sink.
What else is there? I suppose
You can stick it up your nose.
What you can't do I am sad to say
Is consume a Chinese takeaway.

IAN VANNOEY

Sir Alex who?

(opinion polls suggest that most British people have no more than
a passing interest in football (shock horror!))

I have travelled far and my knowledge is quite wide,
But I've never learned or understood the meaning of offside.
Little kids play football because they find it jolly.
Grown-ups play football as they earn lots of lolly.
If you play football you can get your income up.
If your country has loads of dosh you'll stage the World Cup.
Man United is big business; they're quoted on the FTSE.
I have heard they also have a bit to do with footie.
The name David Beckham vaguely rings a bell.
Was not he the chap who married that Spice Girl?
If you're not doing well, and winning is quite hard.
What you have to do is your manager you discard.
If you have been blessed with a really big ego,
You can manage Chelsea like José Mourinho.
In the last World Cup, England had a shocker.
It really doesn't matter, as we're not so keen on soccer.
So if you're fed up with football, and it makes you cross,
You can follow hockey, curling or lacrosse.

26

Alli

Some poems are quite cheerful, others are quite bleak.
This one is about someone who's really quite unique.
She handles everything with efficiency and calm.
When Alli is around there cannot be any harm.
She never has to ask where anything goes,
For, being telepathic, she already knows.
She's painted all my house in brown and green and white.
She'll come and paint a pair of rooms, having worked all night.
She likes nothing better than spending all my lolly.
Most of what she spends, though, makes my house look jolly.
She's very good with children and will play with them all day.
She'll drive many miles, the length of the UK.
The most important quality that Alli has got
Is laughing at my jokes, if they're funny or not.
If you're looking for a home help who is better than Alli then
You won't find one, as she is one in a million.

Things that don't work well on the radio

Radio coverage of ballet
Is rather dull I have to say.
There really isn't much point in waiting
By your radio for figure skating.
Radio schedules are bereft
Of special programmes for the deaf,
Which is why you'll never manage
From the radio to learn sign language.
You're not sorry to have missed
The radio ventriloquist.
If you want a boring time,
Become a fan of radio mime.
Flower shows and aerobatics,
Jugglers and acrobatics.
Tightrope walking, synchronised swimming,
Firework displays and fishing.
If you wish these things to see,
Watch them live or on TV.

Diplospeak (phrases used to describe international negotiations)

What is said	*What this means*
The talks were frank and constructive.	We didn't get anywhere.
The talks will be renewed.	We're still not getting anywhere.
We look forward to an era of enhanced trade and co-operation.	We want your money.
The situation is causing some concern.	We're shit scared.
We shall implement a programme of firm and effective sanctions.	We'll do sod all.
Some progress was made.	No significant progress was made.
All options are on the table.	We haven't the faintest idea what to do.
I raised the issue of human rights.	I wish the issue of human rights would go away.